A YEAR WITH THE
CLAIRVOYANT COACH

Compilation of writings of Libby Pease
HBA ECPC ACC

A Year with a Clairvoyant Coach

Copyright © 2019 Libby Pease

ISBN: 978-1-988215-73-0

Editing and Pre-press:
One Thousand Trees
www.onethousandtrees.com

Printed in M&T Printing Group
Guelph, Ontario

Contents

The Start

By Jerremy Newsom – Real Life Trading LLC

Start small:
Start by doing 1 exercise
Start by drinking 1 cup of water
Start by saving 1 dollar
Start by reading 1 page
Start by buying 1 stock
Start by walking 1 lap
Start by meditating for 1 minute
Start by writing 1 sentence
Start today
Repeat tomorrow
Focus on the process, not the result.
Focus on the process, not the result.
Focus on the process, not the result.
Focus on the process, not the result.
Focus on the process, not the result.
Focus on the process, not the result.

A Year with the Clairvoyant Coach

Since I was very young, I have had a desire to write and share creative thoughts. This creativity has supported me through difficult times and reminded me of the things that matter. Even my dyslexia never dampened my desire to tell a story and share dreams. Within these pages are a compilation of short articles I have written for the local Open Mind Committee and for the people who have followed the unfolding of Listening Tree Studio & Coaching. Some of them are previously published or reworked articles and some can only be found here.

Openly identifying as the Clairvoyant Coach in November of 2019 has been important for me to share the wisdom that has come from my experiences and from my gifts. Many of these articles were written before I came out; however, the wisdom and insight have always been a part of my work.

It doesn't matter at what pace you move towards who you want to be, even one small step or shuffle is movement. Keep believing in your dream and as Jerremy so eloquently stated, "focus on the process, not on the result" because for a long time you will not feel like there are any results. Then one day you will turn around and see how far you have come and how much closer you are to where you want to be.

All of these articles have an element of self-discovery and self-development woven into them. To be honest with you I wrote many as a prompt to reflect on lessons I had already learned but had not been applying or as a reminder of what I needed at the time.

Unlike traditional books where you methodically read from cover to cover, I encourage you to bounce around and read the sections that have most meaning for you at the time you pick up the book. You can, of course, read it straight through as well if you are so inspired. I invite you to pick it up again at times and just see which title catches your eye, as that may be your intuition talking to you and encouraging you to read that section again. One thing I have learned over the years is that you can read a book once and get some value, but when you read it again or multiple times, new layers open to you.

There is also white space for you at the end of each section for you to add sticky notes for your thoughts, ideas and inspirations after reading and digesting the articles.

May this book and all the writings together inspire, soothe and ignite your spark to life!

January

So often there is a lull in the new year when all the excitement of the holidays is put away and we dig into the depths of winter in the northern hemisphere or the scorching heat of summer in the south. It is a great opportunity to hit the reset button and create the balance that you would like to maintain as you move forward.

5 Positive Things to Add to Your Life That Support Balance

When you find yourself in burnout and never really disconnecting from the stress of your life, it's a signal that something is out of balance. To get to a place of balance or a positive life rhythm, you can either remove negative triggers in your life or focus on adding positive things. Adding positive things is our focus today, because "all work and no play" can lead to personal damage.

How to Find a Healthy Balance / Life Rhythm

1. Reconnect with Your Hobbies

    Can you remember when the things you loved doing came first? If you have hobbies, how often are you engaging in those hobbies on your time off? Are these hobbies being set aside because you got a work email, text or a phone call? When we set aside the things that light us up and give us energy, our life rhythm and balance start to tip, and we slide closer to burnout. When you are off from work be present with your personal life! Be present to those activities that bring you joy. Even if things go off the rails at work, be confident in the people you have covering to take care of it.

2. Look Back to the Excitement from Childhood

What were the things that you were excited about as a child or youth? What was the activity you really enjoyed? The activity that you wanted to go out and do with authentic enthusiasm? Something that you felt was yours and fit so well with who you were. This is the place to start to rekindle the passion and build on your authentic self. It is OK if the activity has shifted and changed because you have grown and changed too over the years.

An example is an individual who reminisced, " I used to play guitar in elementary school and high school. Then when I went to university there just didn't seem to be time. I set the guitar aside to work on my grades. Then I started working and I just never got back to it. I really miss playing and jamming with other musicians." The things that you loved when you were younger and had leisure time, those are the things that usually support us and help us recharge. Even if you are not able to connect to a passion from your childhood for whatever reason, ask yourself:

What are other things I've always wanted to do and never had the courage to try?

Do I want to try them now?

This may help to create balance in your life.

3.   Set Boundaries with your Personal Time

How often is it that you don't go to the gym or walk in the woods because someone from work has said, "Well, I may need you between this time and this time," so you just don't go?

When you are off, you are off. When you are on, you are on. It is being present for your personal life as well as for your work life. Balance or a healthy rhythm in life is a challenge especially with all the technology that connects us to the world.

Make time for You so you can recharge your batteries for yourself, the people you love and those you serve with your career!

4.   Real Recharge VS Time Suckers

There are so many things that suck time out of your day; TV, games on our phones or computers, scrolling through social media. Do you feel recharged and rejuvenated after engaging in these activities?

Pay attention to how you feel, and you will know if these activities help to recharge or if they are time suckers. Many individuals will combine a hobby with these activities or make them into social events. For example, knitting or colouring while watching a TV series or networking with other people who game and play together.

5.   Get Support

Finding balance or life rhythm can be difficult! You may need support to find balance. Connecting with a Life Coach that you trust can support you to find the balance that you are seeking. Creating real strategies that honour your life and allow you to be fully present in all elements of your life. It is a gift for you and in turn a blessing to everyone you are linked to!

Article was written in 2018

February

Oh, the February Blahs! Things that weigh us down seem to be amplified at this time of year. Although it is the shortest month of the year, sometimes it appears to drag on longer than all the rest. Loneliness and isolation can be amplified by the weather, lack of sunshine and the lack of activities that take us away from home.

Just Loneliness

Everyone has had the experience of feeling alone and isolated at some point in their lives.

Whether you are living by yourself for the first time or even feeling isolated in a crowd of people, the feeling of loneliness can be present.

For over 20 years I have been the empathetic voice on the other end of a distress line; loneliness and isolation have been the reason behind most of the calls.

I have also been that lonely person who has not reached out because I was afraid of being judged for being "just lonely."

Very few people reach out for support when they are lonely even if that is the root concern for them because it has not been taken seriously.

Loneliness is real. Loneliness is damaging. And we can do something about it. A recent major research study on loneliness in Britain led to the appointment of a Minister of Loneliness, based on the known serious health impacts of loneliness.

It got me thinking and prompted me to look deeper. The study showed that persistent isolation has a higher impact on both physical and mental health than obesity or excessive drinking.

The effects run across the generations from children to the elderly. Isolation should be taken seriously. How often do we eat alone in front of the TV, with computers or other devices? How many opportunities could we take to reduce our own social isolation and that of others?

What can we do? I do most of my work from home and over the internet. It is easy to be days or weeks before I get together with others in person, which is a different interaction for me than the one I have electronically.

Connecting with others in person, sharing time, food and ideas with people who share similar values, culture, and passions is so important.

As an introvert, I am very aware about how I choose to connect with others so that I don't feel like an island in a river of people, keeping in mind the gap between the expectation of what I am looking for in interactions with others and what the reality of the experience actually is. Choosing to have connections with others and arranging to be with others who share things in common with me is something that is meaningful.

When I was a child living in rural Dufferin County, we would go to community dinners, quilting sessions and local fairs.

We would check in regularly with our neighbours who lived alone and invite them to join us when we went to town.

I plan to bring many of these practices back into my life, as well as volunteer and get involved with other local events. Perhaps I'll invite a new neighbour over to have coffee with me.

What are some things you can do that will help alleviate loneliness for yourself and others?

Published in Wellington Advertiser April 12, 2018.

March

March has always been the month of crazy weather, March Break and feeling of cabin fever. It can be a time when individuals tend to take offence quickly or tend to react to their triggers more easily. Had you ever considered that triggers can be your friend? That they are there to let you know of something that is a gift to living a better life? Well, they are. Check out this article that speaks to this.

Gift of Triggers

So often we interpret triggers in our life as negative and bad, as something to be avoided at all costs. What are triggers? Psych Central defines triggers as *"something that sets off a memory tape or flashback transporting the person back to the event of their original trauma. Triggers are very personal; different things trigger different people."* People *"will react to this flashback, trigger with an emotional intensity similar to that at the time of the trauma."* It sounds ghastly and it is horrible when you relive something that had such a huge effect on you in the past. This, of course, is keying into the big triggers. Those are the ones that require supportive therapy to navigate through.

What about the small triggers that are a momentary rush of emotions but don't necessarily affect our regular flow of life?

These are the nagging things that you wish would just stop emerging. The small triggers that we will focus on here. They do provide a gift to us as they show us where we are in our healing journey. They are there for a reason and avoiding them will just cause them to linger longer. So, what is the positive intention behind these? They act as a barometer and a security alarm to keep us safe.

I will give you an example. During my marriage, my husband went to a Live concert to meet up with another woman. When he came back, he played one of their hit songs Lightning Crashes, more times than I could count. I later heard what had transpired during this concert and from then on, that song triggered instant tears, feelings of anger, abandonment, betrayal, unworthiness and pain. This lingered for almost 10 years after.

Today I play the song and enjoy the album it is on. What shifted? I did. The trigger is telling us that there is something within that needs to be addressed. For me, it was the feeling of worthiness. That I am worthy of love, I am worthy of respect, I am worthy of truth. Finding the that core piece and cultivating what I needed for myself shifted the song from a trigger to just a beautiful and creative song. It converted the pain to inner peace. It sounds so simple and it can be, although it is not easy. There was hard work and I sought out support to help me work through this and get to the core of what this trigger was trying to communicate to me.

These small triggers are an indication of when one of our core values has been violated in the moment or when a situation has triggered a memory of when a core value had been dishonoured. When you find yourself triggered take a moment to step back and ask yourself, what does this situation and my reaction to it trying to tell me? What is it that I need to focus on within myself that needs attention?

Knowing what our core values are can help us narrow down an answer to these questions and give us the focus we need for our own healing and self-development.

What triggers would you like to dissipate? What could you enjoy after they are gone?

April

Family can be such a charged subject for people. For some, they are a source of support, love and comfort. For others, they are a source of pain, anguish and anxiety. They can also be a complicated spectrum of all those elements and more.

At the core of family is a group of people who have a shared experience and connection at one point or throughout a person's life. The expectation is that they are there for you, love and support you. That they share the same values and act as a safe refuge from the world. This ideal is not the case for everyone. For so many their blood relations are not safe or they refuse all forms of connection and support. Exile, banishment and shunning have been a form of control in families and societies since the beginning of time and for social creatures like humans, it can be devastating. We are incredibly adaptable creatures and find ways to get our needs met. This article is about recognizing our amazing ability to form new family units with a family of choice when our families of origin can not or will not meet our needs.

There is a quote that has been wildly misinterpreted over the years, "blood is thicker than water." On ThoughtCalalog.com the original quote is *"the blood of the covenant is thicker than the water of the womb"* by Heinrich der Glîchezæreand in 13th century Germany and it expressed the intense bond of soldiers and those who have survived traumatic events. How much more truthful is the original quote and how liberating for those who have had the belief that only blood relatives could have meaningful relationships with them.

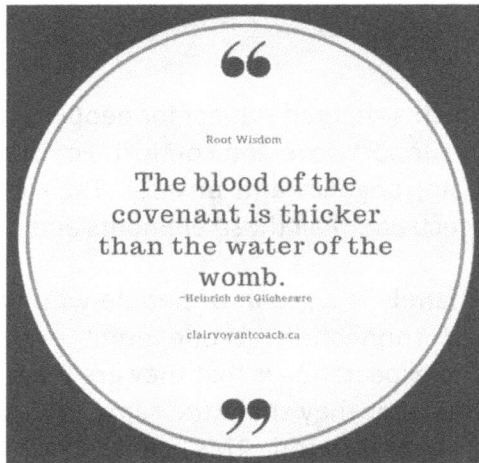

Family – Much More Than Blood

So many of the people I talk to struggle with the idea of family. In most cases, their family is beyond their reach because of religious barriers placed between them and all that is felt is the loss and the void left behind. Even in families where religion has not built walls, there are divides that seem so vast that bridging them seems impossible.

At any time of the year where there is a buzz in the air to gather with family, there are so many individuals that are immobilized by their pain and isolation. This pain is real and is classified as more devastating than the death of someone because of the hope and possibility that the person may change their mind and want to connect.

What I have noticed is that these very same individuals have gathered around them a network of people that have become even closer than the blood relations that so many long for. Family doesn't have to be blood relations. Family can be those we choose to have in our lives.

If this is your situation, I invite you to look around you. Count the friends that you have connected with over the years.

What do you appreciate about each one of them?

What is it about their friendship with you that nourishes you?

What need is met that was left unattended when your family no longer provided it? Or what need is met that your blood family just doesn't possess to provide you?

I am asking these questions of you because what you may be seeking may already be around you in your circle of friends. Now I know that for many friends will not wholly replace the relative they are missing. Chosen family through our friends can support us with elements that we crave and provide even more than we ever expected. Things like connection, loyalty, under-standing, affection, trust, an empathetic ear, companionship, and so much more.

One suggestion in my Reclaim Your Power – Shunning Recovery course is to build and maintain friendships to fill the needs that are being neglected when shunned by close family members. So many have already built friendships yet have not fully grasped how beneficial this is when we choose to adopt and accept our trusted friends as family.

How many friends do you have now that could move into the status of family for you?

May

I have always been fascinated with dreams and the insight that they give us. During elementary school, I am sure my teacher thought I was doing drugs because of the strange creative writing projects I would submit that were based on the dreams that I had. Later, I realized that my dreams had more to them than just creative writing material. I have had visions of what later happened in the future, had insight into what was going on for those around me and been able to work out major issues with creative solutions inspired by the journeys in my dreams.

This article touches on this and talks about not only the importance of sleep but also the importance of dreaming.

Dream, Perspective and Sleep

So many of the articles that I write about healing have the element of sleep involved in them. However, sleep is just one element of that equation. The other elements are the release into dreaming and the benefits of what dreaming does for your mental and overall health.

For this piece I did a bit of research as my experience with dreams is on the side of dream analysis, dreams as part of my clairvoyance and dreams as being a beautiful way to take a new perspective on what is happening in your life.

So, what do the experts say about dreaming? WebMD talks a bit about the debate of what dreams are. Some describe it as a "by-product of sleep" while others feel that it is important to filing and processing memories and coping with emotions. All levels of sleep can produce dreams but the REM (Rapid Eye Movement) or deep sleep is the most significant. Dreams are easiest to recall immediately after waking, so if you wish to capture your dreams it is suggested to record your dream either verbally or by writing in a journal that is immediately ready and handy beside your bed. If you get up to find materials the dream has time to dissipate like smoke in the wind. One thing that has been noticed by researchers is that individuals tend to wake up with solutions or ideas that may benefit something that was an issue for the person. Dreams allow us to take all the pieces of our life that we are dealing with and put them together in a new and creative way. Essentially allowing us to take a different perspective and disassociate (watch from and outside view) to see the situation without the emotional charge that it may possess while awake.

There are some interesting studies through the National Sleep Foundation (also from WebMD) that suggest that dreaming can help to alleviate depression. However, alcohol and substance use can affect a person's ability to dream. In a June 2009 article in Psychology Today, they sited that when individuals used substances they did not dream, and had less deep sleep called REM sleep. This lack of dreaming, more than the loss of sleep, have been associated with decline in health, increased depression and difficulty in thought processing. When they no longer consumed alcohol or other substances the individuals had a flood of dreams and the other negative effects started to reverse.

It is the dreaming part of sleep that heals us. It is a form of decluttering, organizing and way of aligning ourselves with what really matters in life. It allows us to take our issues and organize them in a different way and from a new perspective.

For me, dreams have been a way of finding clarity. From very young I would have lucid dreams, which are vivid dreams that I knew I was dreaming. I wasn't just watching the dream; I could be active in it as well. These have been the most powerful dreams for me. If they repeated over three nights or more, I knew that they had elements I needed to pay attention to as they would have a bearing on my life.

I will give you an example. After the death of an important family member of mine, I inherited craft supplies along with projects that remained unfinished. The first night after I received the supplies, I had a dream of this person. They demanded I finish the projects and give them to specific people. Understandable to have such a dream given the circumstances and having a sense of obligation to complete unfinished items. The next night I started to have the same dream, but this time I spoke to this person to get a better understanding of what needed to be done and for whom. This continued until the projects were completed. Then the dream shifted to instructions on the recipients and some impatience on the person's part for my not delivering them immediately. Once the items were finished these dreams stopped and went back to the dream patterns I had had before.

My therapist friends would say that this is tied to my subconscious and my feelings of obligation given to me by this relative. My woo-woo friends would say it is the dead speaking with me from the other side to ensure I finished their work so they could rest.

For me, I feel it is a bit of both. I know that when I dream I can find some amazingly creative solutions to things that have felt unsolvable. That taking the time to analyse them can open new insights that support understanding and growth. I also know that dreams help to see the deeper part of me that helps to be whole, accepting the flattering and unflattering parts of myself and presenting the authentic me. I also know that I have become privy to information that I was not exposed to in waking, which has had an impact on myself and people in my life!

What is dreaming for you? How will knowing that dreaming has a positive impact on your overall health change your sleep habits?

June

What a wonderful month that June is.

Spring is flowing into summer and everything is really starting to grow. It is finally a time to enjoy the outdoors and pack away the cares of the past few months. One of my favourite things to do is to actually stand outside in the first warm rain and just let the rain fall over me. Let it wash away the stress, worry and cares that I have been lugging around with me for so long.

It is also my birth month. This means releasing what is no longer supportive to me from the past year so that I am fresh and open to all the things that can help me over the next year. It is a spring cleaning of your soul really. How much better do you feel when your space is cleaned of clutter and everything is in its place for you to use?   Internally you need this too. Look at these ways to help you to release the internal clutter.

5 Ways to Release

When people think of release this could be the release of stress, the release of worry, the release of feeling like a victim, or release of anything that is weighing you down or keeping you from being fully available to yourself and others. It can be anything that is no longer serving you.

1. Breathe

    The best advice from my mother gave me was to remember to breathe. As a kid, you don't want to take any advice from your parents, but this one always stuck with me. When I was stressed, anxious or scared I tended to hold my breath. This, of course, would make things worse. You can't think or act when you are not breathing. I know when I did end up taking a breath I was a blubbering mess. A great quote from Fredrick Solomon Perls is "Fear is excitement without the breath." So, remember to breathe.

2. Move

    I don't mean a move to a new house or move to a different city or country, even though that could be a part of it. I mean physically move. Move your body by having a walk, going to the gym, yoga, swimming, mime, dancing, Monty Python silly walk – anything that allows movement of your body. Do something different from what you usually do. That movement can shift the energy for you and thereby allow you to release.

3. Meditation/Mindfulness

I know these have been buzz words for a while, but they really do work. When you are stressed or worried or carrying something, you tend to ruminate on that piece constantly. With meditation or mindfulness, you are giving your mind a rest from the hamster wheel of information buzzing around your head. Shifting to giving your brain space to relax and watch the clouds go by can help to shift perspective once you are done. Meditation and mindfulness also focus on the breath so you would be able to get two for the price of one. You can release by allowing your mind to stop, rest and relax.

4. Do something you love

How often do you do something that you love? I don't mean the latest video game on your phone. I mean something that gives you joy and really fills you up. So often for the sake of all the other priorities in our lives, we give up or set aside the things that give us joy. Is there a hobby you used to have but haven't done for a long time? Is there a place you used to always visit that even if you were there for only an hour it felt like a vacation for your soul? The world tends to give us the message that we must work harder, but when we bring joy back to our lives it really can shift everything else and allow us to have the resilience and capacity to move forward. This is a prescription to do what you love for the long-term benefits it provides.

5.   Sleep

One of the first things to go when we are stressed is sleep. This can be a difficult one to control as many who live with insomnia can attest to. It is also one of the most beneficial in providing release. When your mind can rest, and rest for longer than your time with meditation or mindfulness, some of those things that are stressors and felt like unscalable mountains can shift to being more manageable. Sleep gives you the ability to process so much more then your conscious mind can focus on. It allows details to float and shift perspective and land in patterns we would never have thought of when awake. When you dream you are also able to detach the emotion from the situation and this gives space for new possibilities. Give yourself that space to sleep.

Which of these ways are you most likely to try first to release something in your life?

July

July is the time of summer camp and long summer days that seem to drift on and on. There could be summer vacations and trips to the cottage or road trips for the sake of adventure. How often do our everyday lives follow us? In this digital age, it is so easy to take work with you. It follows us in our pockets. Our colleagues may think that just one call will be OK, even if you are on vacation or holidays. What impact does that have on us? How many times have you seen friends or family members lugging around computers and multiple phones during their vacations? Or watched other vacationers at resorts trying desperately to find those 2 bars of cell service so they can send just one more email, text or document. Is this really taking time off? Is this what time off is being accepted as today?

For July I have actually added two articles about unplugging from work and finding the benefits of being present in what you are doing and who you are with when you are on vacation. The strong message here is:

When you are off, unplug!

Unplug to Find the Stillness

Consider in a day how often you are unplugged from technology. Living in rural Ontario, I have woken up in the morning with the power out and really been surprised by the absolute stillness. No hum or click of devices. This silence can be disconcerting for many. Why? We are so conditioned to always being plugged in with the TV, computer, phone or radio on and being barraged by sound from all directions. It is rare that we find ourselves in stillness and hear what lays in the silence.

There are great benefits to unplugging and taking some time to be still.

1. You give your mind time to relax.

    Constant stimulation from technology tends to have us live in a constantly "ON" or anxious state. When you unplug and be in the stillness, your mind can then have time to relax (to begin with it may be more anxious from withdrawal; however, this will shift as you ease into it).

2. There is an increased awareness.

   Let's say you go for a walk and you decide not to pick up your phone or turn on a podcast or music. As you walk, what do you start noticing about your surroundings? What do you notice about your thoughts? What would you have missed if you were still plugged in?

3. There is an increase in self-awareness and intuition.

   So often we have the world up so loud that we can not or do not hear what we say to ourselves or what our inner voice and intuition are saying. When we unplug and get used to the stillness, we become more aware of our self-talk and have the power to shift it. We also are more in tune with our intuition. It is no longer fighting to be heard over the clamour.

   What benefits will you find when you unplug?

"Unplugging" – Necessary for Self-Care (2012)

Have you ever gone away for vacation and ended up doing more work for your job than relaxing for yourself? Technology is constantly advancing and allowing us to do more on smaller and more accessible devices; consequently, we have the ability to connect to the office computer from our computer at home. This is great during office hours because it allows us to be away from the office but still be "connected." The downfall of this convenience is that you are ALWAYS "connected." Your coworkers, clients and industry partners become used to relying on you to receive their call or email and come to expect you to respond at any time of day even if you are on vacation.

In my personal life as well as in my career I enjoy staying connected. My phone has internet access and at one time, both my personal and work email came directly to it. I always knew what was going on, even when travelling out east on vacation, or as I left civilization for a canoe trip. But the cost of staying connected can become a burden for your emotional and mental health.

I remember an instance where I was due to go on a weeklong canoe trip with my teenage daughter. I was anxious about going out of cell phone range "just in case." "What if there is an emergency at the office?" "What if the volunteers don't show up?" Of course, I had back up people covering all of this, but letting go and trusting that everything will be covered was difficult.

It turned out that there was an emergency, but I had been out of cell phone range for over 24 hours. Once I was in range my cell phone had bells and whistle go off with emails and voice mails set to high priority. I instantly went into work mode in the middle of Smoke Lake – Algonquin Park. My daughter looked at me like I was an alien as I made phone calls and tried to follow up. I became more and more anxious since I could not reach anyone. It dawned on me that I was at least an hour paddle from the shore and another 45 minutes from my car than a six-hour drive to the office. We were only halfway through our vacation week and just coming out to pick up another member of the trip. When we got to shore my daughter took my phone, removed the battery and locked both in separate cars.

She said, "This is our time. Enjoy your vacation in the bush. The office will still be there next week." And you know what? She was right. Now when I am not at work or on-call I avoid checking my work email and when I am on vacation I focus on my friends and family rather than obsessing over what is happening at the office. It is always "there" when I get back – after I have had a chance to really unwind, relax and take care of myself.

This article was written by Elizabeth Pease, former Volunteer & Community Coordinator for Community Torchlight – Distress Centre for Wellington and Dufferin Counties for the Open Mind column. She has been a part of the Distress Line movement since 1996. Originally written in January 2012.

August

So much and yet so little happens in the month of August. It is the last month of summer and everyone strives to get the most of it. It is the time that all the seeds you planted in your gardens are fully grown and producing. There is an exchange of produce for those who tend gardens. It is also the last weeks or month of summer holidays for the kids before they go back to school. The one thing that I look forward to the most is the music! Each August we trek up to Owen Sound for Summerfolk – Music and Crafts Festival. It is a chance to connect with people you see every year and to enjoy amazing music from all over. Music has a powerful effect on us. It can bring us to every emotion and soothe our soul.

Music that Heals the Soul

I remember when my daughter was very young. To soothe her to sleep I would often sing a lullaby I heard from the TV show Cheers. She would call it her Lura Song and I believe it is the Irish Lullaby by James Shannon and made widely known by Bing Crosby. Music has the power to draw out many emotions and link us in an instant to memories from our past.

Back when I started at the University of Windsor, I had the opportunity to volunteer at the Alzheimer's Society's Day Away

Program. This program provided a safe place for individuals who suffered from Alzheimer's and other forms of dementia. We would do many activities throughout the day, but the one thing that really rekindled the joy on their faces is when we would play music from their youth. You could see the shift in their energy and all the memories would fill them with joy. When I listen to the Andrews Sisters – Boogie Woogie Bugle Boy I can see the group totally get into it. These songs had the power to bring them to a different time and bring them to joy. This feeling would stay with them for the rest of the day.

As children of the 70's and 80's, we would make mixed tapes for our friends and anyone that we may have had a crush on. These tapes would try to relay in music what we could not express in words.

Music is an expression, but can it also heal?   In the February 2014 article in Psychology Today "Does Music Have Healing Powers?" they sited that there is research to show that music, in fact, does heal. Music therapy has shown improvements on mood disorders and chronic pain. It isn't just the melody, but the lyrics can have an effect too with positive verses shifting the moods and perspectives of those who listen to them. The converse is also true. Harsh songs and hateful lyrics can spiral individuals into dark places.

New research is being done on the effects of certain frequencies of sounds and their effect on healing or motivating us. On the RationalWik there is information about the Solfeggio Frequencies which were considered as healing frequencies. The most recognizable of these are the tones found in the Sound of Music song Do Re Mi. I know that when I listen to music composed with these frequencies as their structure that my work is more focused, more clearly flows and even with a busy day, I feel accomplished and energized.

What effects does music have for you?

What do you notice about your playlists and your moods after you listen to them?

Being mindful of the music that we choose to surround ourselves with can influence how we feel and what we do. Knowing that it is so powerful can allow us to actively choose and utilize it as part of our healing journey.

How will this knowledge shift the way you choose and listen to music?

September

After Labour Day it is time to get back to the swing of things with work and school. We dive into projects and leave behind the fun and sun. So many of us are burning the candle at both ends to catch up or to be everything to everyone. This is a good time to be reminded that we are not islands. We can create supportive networks to share the load for all of us as we move forward in life.

Help the Healer – Network of Pillars

I was inspired to write this article last week and jotted down the points I wanted to make. There are days when inspiration hits you from all sides and you do your best to jot the ideas as they come fast and intense. These inspirations really sink in on the days where nothing seems to click, like today, and you realize how much value was written in those few scribbled notes.

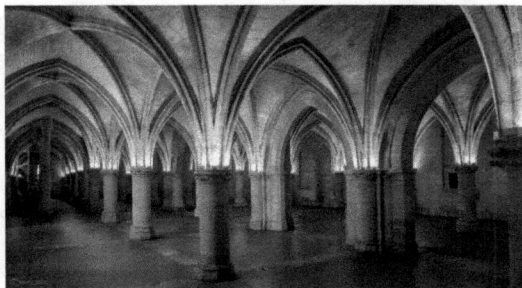

Those who are there when we are down, hurt or in a panic are healers on so many levels. They slow down, give you all the time in the world, seek to understand and do their best to support you to a better place. What happens to them when they are down, hurt or in a panic? I know from my 20 years of experience working in crisis response that first responders and other healers struggle to seek out help, even though they are keenly aware of its value. Why is this? The individual may be afraid that seeking help will impact how others see their ability to do their job. They may perceive it as a sign of weakness or just feel they don't have the time to help themselves when so many others need the help more.

I can sympathize with this from my own experiences. As a volunteer and assistant trainer at the Distress Centre for Windsor Essex, I was drowning myself in shifts and extra training events. My home life was falling apart and the work of training volunteers and helping those on the phones gave me a false sense of purpose when my life at home was devoid of meaning. This happened again many years later as a full-time manager and trainer at Community Torchlight when funding was being pulled and there were huge shifts and pressures along with personal challenges with mental health with members of my household. There were huge pressures, huge overwhelm and a fear that if I admitted I needed help I would lose respect, lose my job, and it made more sense in my stressed mind to find a way to get hurt so I would have a valid reason to escape real life and rest for a while. In both cases, I was fortunate enough to have people who recognized that something was wrong. My deepest gratitude goes to both Sybil Lowry and Katherine Johnson for being the people who stepped up when I was burning out.

This is happening for others. I am not an isolated case. Our network of supports are all burning out and suffering from compassion fatigue everywhere and the system is not set up in a way to give us what we need to fully get back on our feet. We need to find a way to create a safe space for healers to reach out and support each other so they can take the essential time to recharge and find their footing again. What I envision is a network of healer pillars in overlapping arches so when we need it we can step away and know our load is supported by the entire network around us. The network creating a space that allows full recovery so we can come back and take our space again. This would be with safe people to talk to. Those who will hold the space for you and support you to find what you need to go from empty to full.

For people who work in their own private practice, consider joining or creating a peer support group that can be a safe place to connect, work as a sounding board for challenges you are having in your own business or with your clients, and a place to gain connection and emotional support.

Having my own independent practise I have the flexibility on a day that doesn't flow to be able to move away from my desk, meditate, contact my supports, be in nature and all of the other things that I know will heal me so I can be fully present for those I support. This is not the case for everyone. What I am proposing here is an opportunity to create this network of overlapping arches to be that safe place to support those who are looking for a safe place, because we all need someone to lean on so we can Live Strong and Authentic Lives and not just smile and fake it.

October

As Canadians, we have our Thanksgiving in October. It is a time when families get together and share the food and for some, it is a time of gratitude for all that the summer has yielded in their gardens and on their farms. There are many Thanksgivings that my garden was what gave us the bounty to celebrate when funds were tight.

Gratitude is so powerful though and this article really draws into how it can support you throughout the year and not just in October or November during Thanksgiving.

Be Thankful
Show Appreciation
Return Kindness

Gratitude

Gratitude: More Than Just the Season

It is now October, the month when we celebrate Thanksgiving. It is a season that reminds us to think about what we are thankful and grateful for.

But what is gratitude and how can it shift how we live our lives? I looked up the definition of gratitude and found it includes three important elements:

1. Being thankful
2. Ready to show appreciation
3. Willing to return kindness

I was a bit surprised by this third element. Certainly, being thankful and showing appreciation were in my thoughts about gratitude but, being willing to return kindness expands this concept so much further.

About a year ago I was strongly encouraged to start a gratitude journal and write down 10 things I was grateful for every day. At first, I felt like it was sort of a punishment, having to write outlines of what I was grateful for. I recalled It was like having to write lines on the board for chewing gum in class when I was a kid.

Soon, though, I came to recognize that it was more than just making a list. It became a way to remember at least 10 things in every day that I experienced and thought about and was thankful for. It was a way to show appreciation through my pen and then also remember to show appreciation to those who showed me kindness. And it was a reminder for me to be kind to others so that they could have something to add to their gratitude journal.

Don't get me wrong! There are some days where finding one thing, let alone 10 things can be extremely difficult, but consider this. When you have those challenging days and get through them, what have you gained? What have you learned about yourself that you may not have known before? What positive things did you learn about others that you had not noticed before? There can be some amazing insights from challenging days that you may never have noticed before if you were not looking for elements to be grateful for.

Another piece to gratitude is the shift in perspective. You may have heard of the adage that you get more of what you focus on. Well, that is very true when it comes to gratitude. If you are searching through your day for things to be thankful for you will learn how to find them. As you find them you will notice that there are more things in your life to be grateful for. The mind is an amazing thing. It wants to please you and find what it is you are looking for.

Practising regular gratitude in my daily life has made a huge shift in how I see the world and appreciate things around me. Actually allowing myself to feel the gratitude as I put pen to paper has made the process powerful and motivates me to continue. I also found that there was a huge difference writing my gratitude journal with pen and paper rather than on the computer.

How do you think regular gratitude might shift your life?

November

November combines the solemnness of Remembrance Day with the ramping up of Christmas and for our American neighbours the celebration of Thanksgiving. November of 2019 was a pivotal point for me where I peeled back another layer in my own development and willingness to show up as who I authentically am. Being authentic is a continual process of growth, revealing your true self and then letting the world know. It doesn't happen all at once.

Stepping into yourself can be the most terrifying and liberating thing you can do in your life. It can happen more than once. What would you need to take those leaps to live your authentic life?

> Sometimes deciding who you are is deciding who you'll never be again.
>
> Unknown

Authentic Life

Imagine a life where you can be your full, free and authentic self. Even thinking about it is a challenge for most of us because Real-Life can squash even dreaming of it. Roles that we have been assigned by our family, society and even ourselves often stifle imagining much less actually making dreams a reality. How can we live authentic lives?

What would it mean for you to set aside the present reality of your life and allow yourself to dream? Through my life, I have been encouraged and moved outside of my comfort zone and allowed myself not only to dream but bring my dreams into reality. Now I support others to do just this in my role as a Life Coach.

Growing up my parents let me do the "boyish" stuff that I enjoyed but I was always reminded that I was a girl and was to behave as such. I remember being raised with the impression that in my family boys were of higher value. I wanted to be out there working with machinery. I wanted to be in work boots, lugging wood and swearing up a storm with the boys.

What made this divide even more distinct for me was my choice to convert to a very strict fundamentalist religion and marry a man who valued very traditional roles. As wife and mother, I (needed to be) was expected to be submissive as well as dress and act appropriately. As you can imagine this caused much mental anguish and led to depression, illness and suppressed anger.

There was a pivotal day that turned everything around for me. I remember distinctly that I was in my kitchen, having a heated discussion with my husband. I had a glass pot in my hand, full of spaghetti sauce. I remember turning around and yelling "ENOUGH!" and smashed the glass pot on the counter. I shattered the pot and that part of my life. This wasn't just "Enough" to my marriage, but also to the lifestyle I had been living and denying who I was.

Over the next 15 years, I had the honour of working with many mentors and coaches who supported me to open to my true self. I was able to find a way to live as my authentic self. I am a proud, strong, intelligent, outspoken woman, who enjoys cutting wood with chainsaws and building with power tools and who can tear up and show a vulnerable side too.

I am an entrepreneur who wears comfortable shoes and speaks powerfully at presentations and conferences. I live my authentic life and I can now help others too.

December

Oh, the Christmas Buzz is in the air steeped with expectations and traditions. There is so much pressure to be joyful and giving. This can be so stressful when you don't have the finances, emotional or physical capacity to fulfil these expectations.

One thing that has struck me about those who may be creating their first Christmas after leaving a community that doesn't celebrate Christmas is, there are no deep traditions restricting their capacity to be creative. Now I know there is also stress there on how to do this thing people call Christmas, but when you don't care what others think or have no one pressuring you with expectations you can have some really magical and authentic ideas.

Really it is a reminder to all of us that we don't have to have a movie perfect Christmas. Just the one that feels right for us.

5 Ways to Service Your Holiday Stress

So many people find themselves stressed over the holidays trying to meet some pretty fantastic expectations. Just like your car or snow blower may need a tweak or full servicing as the seasons change. Here are 5 ideas to support you this holiday.

1. If your decorations are not up by a week before Christmas, then it is OK to leave them in the box for another year!

   a. Only put up what feels right for you.
   b. It doesn't have to be the same every year.

2. Make Christmas Dinner a potluck!

   a. This can be a surprise about what people bring.
   b. It can be prearranged who makes what.
   c. There is more time to socialize rather than one or two people stuck in the kitchen.

3. Have few presents or none at all.

   a. Handmade gifts that you have created over the year.
   b. One thing that is meaningful.
   c. Donate to a charity in the name of someone on your list.
   d. Proclaim a gift free holiday with an abundance of food and great company.

4. Delegate

   a. You don't have to do it all. Give others a task to do and accept how that task is once completed.

5. Self-Care

   a. Self-care is the pause you give yourself. The permission to stop when things START feeling like they are too much.
   b. Take a walk.
   c. Call a friend.

d. Play a game.
e. Find something that makes you laugh.
f. Read a book.

My uncle once reminded me how my aunt used to get herself in a knot when hosting at the holidays and it would take her a week after to recover. When I took on the reigns his advice was to not sweat it. Even if the food fails and the decorations are eaten by the cat, those who truly love you will enjoy being in your company and probably tell the story as a beloved holiday family classic!

Oh if someone has an issue with the way you have chosen to celebrate this year, they have automatically nominated themselves to host next year!

Wishing you a Very Happy and Enjoyable Holidays!

In Appreciation

We have now come to the end. This has been a wonderful journey bringing together articles that I have written over the years and creating new ones just for here.

I would like to thank a few people that made this all happen. First I would like to thank Lia Dunlap – the Oracle On Purpose for all of our work together over the past few years that brought me to a place where I can more widely let my light shine. Thank you to Lady Shadow Raven for being direct and encouraging and giving me that solid nudge to really start writing in a meaningful way again.

Thank you to Myles for being my in house editor and for all your support as I build my practice.

Thank you Meagen for being the catalyst that inspired me to be more.

And finally Thank you, Lisa, for taking a chance on this book.

About the Author

Libby Pease, Internationally Certified Coach and 20-year crisis response expert, and Clairvoyant specializing in cult recovery with Listening Tree Studio & Coaching. She draws on her experience of helping people in crisis to supporting individuals to be proactive and really step into who they are. Thereby creating a life that is meaningful and increasing their ability to cope with life's challenges.

Libby specializes in supporting individuals who have emerged from highly controlling communities, religions, families, relationships and workplaces; who are committed to moving forward in their lives; shifting the shame, guilt and isolation to clarity, confidence and joy!

Her unique life purpose is to be the clairvoyant who lights the path for those who will change the world.

www.clairvoyantcoach.ca
Belwood, ON
Canada